YOUR KNOWLEDGE HAS VALUE

Bibliographic information published by the German National Library:

The German National Library lists this publication in the National Bibliography; detailed bibliographic data are available on the Internet at http://dnb.dnb.de .

Imprint:

Copyright © 2016 GRIN Verlag
Print and binding: Books on Demand GmbH, Norderstedt Germany
ISBN: 9783668156838

This book at GRIN:

https://www.grin.com/document/315743

Andrea Attwenger

The crime forecasting process. Application, critique and discussion

GRIN Verlag

GRIN - Your knowledge has value

Since its foundation in 1998, GRIN has specialized in publishing academic texts by students, college teachers and other academics as e-book and printed book. The website www.grin.com is an ideal platform for presenting term papers, final papers, scientific essays, dissertations and specialist books.

Visit us on the internet:

http://www.grin.com/

http://www.facebook.com/grincom

http://www.twitter.com/grin_com

Ludwig-Maximilians-Universität München

Institut für Informatik

Wintersemester 2015/16

Seminar und Praktikum Wissenschaftliches Arbeiten und Lehren

Crime forecasting

Andrea Attwenger

Master Medieninformatik, 1. Fachsemester

Abstract

The development of new information systems and data mining techniques has made it possible to make predictions of the place, time, victim or perpetrator of a future crime by analyzing past crime reports.

Providing that enough relevant data has been collected before, computational algorithms can be used to find patterns and forecast crimes. Underlying theories make use of criminological findings such as the increased threat to areas already targeted once or to areas close to a victimized neighborhood.

The usage of computers allows for a quicker and more effective analysis as well as the discovery of patterns otherwise not humanly detectable. In order to be effective, forecasts need to be followed by concrete measures. They can be used to plan police operations and specifically deploy forces and resources in realtime.

This paper describes the most important steps of the crime forecasting process.

Index Terms—Crime forecasting, predictive policing, near-repeat theory

CONTENT

I. INTRODUCTION

A man is arrested for a crime he has not even committed yet. This scene straight out of Philip K. Dick's famous novel "Minority Report" could soon become reality with the introduction of computational crime forecasting in everyday policing. Of course no one is going to get prematurely arrested, but police departments and computer scientists are working on ways to forecast felonies and stop them from even happening.

The field of predictive policing applies analytic techniques in order to identify areas or individuals at risk, to then specifically deploy forces and resources and therefore to crime risk or even solve past crimes [1], [2]. These analytic techniques do not have to be computational, but the usage of computers and algorithms considerably eases data collection, storage and representation. Additionally, computational methods might show patterns that would otherwise not be obvious to a human analyst [3].

A single felony will always be basically unpredictable, as it does not take place regularly or at a predefined time and place [3], [4]. However, it is possible to find patterns of crimes related to a specific neighborhood, season or to other characteristics by analyzing past crime reports. Police data shows that criminals respond to opportunities and habit. On the one hand, they are attracted badly protected neighborhoods as well as disorderly areas with already high crime levels, both signaling a good opportunity for committing crimes without being caught. On the other hand, offenders often return to their crime scene or even repeatedly continue to commit crimes within the same area. [4], [5]

The goal of predictive policing is to exploit these patterns in order to effectively allocate or adjust patrols and other resources, and therefore to "transform policing from a reactive process to a proactive process" [3]. Police officers should not be forced to just react to 911 calls, but instead communicate with citizens and create an ordered environment that stops crimes from even happening [6], [7].

The rest of the paper is structured as follows: In section II, the analytic steps of the crime forecasting process are presented. Firstly, the generation of data, comprising the collection and representation of relevant information, is described in section II-A. Following this, several predictive methods are introduced in section II-B. Section III gives information on the application of predictive policing and the interventions and operations that ideally follow crime forecasting methods. Eventually, potential pitfalls and points of criticism, like over-reliance on predictive methods or a lack of transparency, are described in section IV. In section V, the paper concludes with a summary of the most important points and an outlook to further developments.

II. THE CRIME FORECASTING PROCESS

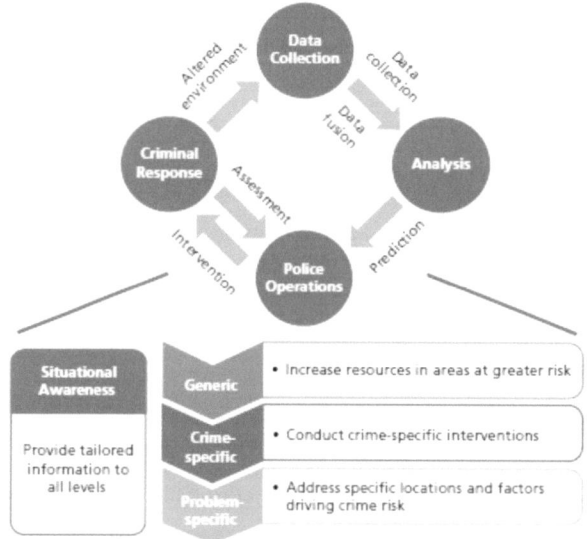

Fig. 1. The four-step predictive process according to Perry et al. in [1].
Data is being collected and analyzed, then the resulting predictions are used
to plan police operations (e.g. increasing resources, adjustment of patrols)
accordingly. The criminal response to these interventions creates new data
that is being fed into the database anew.

Analyzing data and discovering patterns is not everything in the crime forecasting process. For the predictions to be useful, the specific police department has to act on them. The process can be described as a four-step cycle, as shown in figure 1.

The first two steps are concerned with the classical data treatment: Reams of data of past events, concerning the type of crime, the exact time and place and maybe other useful identifiers, are being fed into a database and analyzed for patterns. The results of these examinations might be used to conduct spot-on interventions in areas at risk or to simply adjust existing patrols. [1], [3]

A. *Data generation*

The quality of predictions depends strongly on the quality of the data used to make them [1]. Crime data and maps have to be up date, containing the very latest events , in order to be useful for analysis and forecasting [5]. The collected data is then preprocessed and represented in a model designed to facilitate pattern recognition in the desired resolution.

1) Collecting information:

Most of the data used by computational forecasting systems is also being collected in standard police procedures. Police agencies have been mapping crimes using geographic information systems and adding additional information for a long time, in order to better discover and understand criminal patterns [8], [9]. The data necessary for predictive analytics is therefore already there and databases can be fed with many years of past events.

The collected information for each event usually contains the type of crime, the location and the time of the incident, sometimes also additional information like attributes of the targeted property or individual [4]. Using this data, seasonal or geographical frequency counts of crimes can be made and utilized to identify hot spots (see II-B1) and potentially forecast crimes [8].

2) Data representation:

Before any analyzing of the collected information can begin, the data needs to be preprocessed and properly represented. Yu et al. [4] divided a geographical area into grid cells of at one point one-half, at another point one-quarter mile square and populated these cells with monthly data on occurring crimes. The monthly data is a matrix of six categories of felonies. Mu et al.'s approach [9] using a fourth-order tensor encoding longitude, latitude, time and other relevant events amounts to a similar outcome, since they also divide the city into grid cells for a more feasible localization.

Choosing the right grid resolution for the respective neighborhood is crucial for the quality of predictions and the success of the overall process. On the one hand, the separate cells have to be small enough to allow the effective deployment of forces and implementation of operations [1], [10] (see also figure 2). On the other hand, adding too much information to a fine-grained grid leads to a model that does not yield usable patterns but says nothing definitive at all [3]. Yu et al. [4] researched two different resolutions of grid cells and found out that the lower resolution led to better predictive results.

B. Predictive analytics

Making predictions based on existing data is a method instinctively used by police officers. However, studies have showed that model-based algorithms are far more accurate in forecasting crimes than traditional police practices [10].

The reason why predictive methods can work is that crimes such as residential burglaries or car thefts are usually influenced by a number of different factors. These factors can be characteristics of the area, but also of the surrounding landscape [11]. Generally speaking, areas that have already fallen victim to crimes, as well as their adjoining neighborhoods are especially at risk to be targeted (again) [5]. By identifying hot spots of crime occurrence and areas at risk based on their unique characteristics, and then looking at their surrounding neighbors, a lot of reliable predictions can be made [4], [9].

1) Hot spot identification:

Hot spot identification is a basic functionality of most crime prediction algorithms. A predefined area is being scanned in order to identify clusters with high levels of crime occurrence, the so-called hot spots [12]. The simple underlying assumption being that "the hot spots of yesterday are the hot spots of tomorrow" [13]. According to Gorr et al., hot spots usually combine several crime indicators: "(1) motivated offenders, (2) suitable targets, and (3) the absence of a capable guardian" [10]. By identifying these hot spots and then specifically deploying patrols there, the third of these conditions and subsequently the other two can be eliminated.

The emergence of more developed mapping and visualization technologies has made it easier to track the evolution and displacement of these hot spots and monitor areas of concern outside traditional policing boundaries [12], [14]. However, in developing algorithms for hot spot prediction, one must consider the prevalence of cold spots in the overall observed area. By weighting cold and hot spots equally, the model would get better trained to recognize areas without crimes than the desired areas at risk. That is to say, the weight of the hot spots needs to be enhanced – despite the overall accuracy sinking - in order to train an algorithm that focuses on hot spot prediction. [4]

2) Risk-terrain modeling:

The aforementioned hot spot identification method is very much determined by previous crimes piling up and forming a hot spot. Risk terrain modeling is centered more on the interaction of social, physical, geographical or behavioral factors occurring at a specific place. Examples for these indicators are the residential location of individuals already arrested for committing felonies in the past, the proximity of quick escape routes or the demographic concentration of young males. [15] Also the existence of bus stops, public housing, bars, liquor stores, fast food restaurants and even schools was found to be correlated with violent crimes [16].

Similarly to the hot spot approach, risk-terrain modeling can also be used to adjust police operations and patrols in order to protect potentially endangered areas.

3) The near-repeat theory:

Near repeat theory postulates the assumption that once a crime has happened at a specific place, this particular location and its surrounding environments are more likely to be subjects to additional, subsequent crimes [1], [15]. The pattern of crime infecting adjacent areas and therefore spreading through a neighborhood like a contagious disease can be compared to the occurrence of earthquakes. It is well known for initial earthquakes to trigger aftershocks in the surrounding area; this model of "self-exciting point processes" was modified by Mohler et al. in [17] for the purpose of crime modeling.

According to Ferguson [15], data supports the near-repeat phenomenon for property-based crimes such as residential burglaries; two theories have been produced in order to explain this effect. Flag theory follows a hypothesis similar to the assumptions behind risk terrain modeling (see II-B2) and broken windows theory (see II-B4): crimes repeatedly happen at similar places because criminals respond to the same signs, such as disorder, target vulnerability or target attractiveness. According to boost theory, however, the act of committing a crime allows the offender to learn information that enhances the vulnerability of the area, such as burglars breaking into a house and thereby becoming familiar to the weaknesses of neighboring houses as well.

In their exploration of data mining techniques for crime forecasting, Yu et al. [4] apply the near-repeat theory combined with a usage of temporal data. Employing the so-called "t-Month Approach", they describe crimes happening in one month by previous counts of crimes in the months before. Moreover, they try to gain spatial knowledge by employing different classifiers. The baseline is the One Nearest Neighbor algorithm that simply assumes that "similar circumstances must result in similar outcomes". Spatially constrained, this algorithm establishes that an area targeted once is more likely to fall victim to a crime again. The authors further use classifiers such as a decision tree, neural networks and naive Bayes, with Bayes yielding the best prediction results with an accuracy between 70 and 80%.

4) The broken windows theory:

The near-repeat theory estimates occurrences of crimes nearby as an indicator for future crimes. The broken windows theory follows a similar direction, but starts even sooner: it claims that even small signs of disorder disturb a community and invite criminals.

That is to say, that mess or disorderliness and crime are closely correlated. The eponymous "broken windows" have to be instantly repaired, or else further destruction and subsequently the decline of the whole neighborhood will follow. [6] Applying this effect on forecasting models means not only integrating factual crimes, but also potential indicators of disorder, such as physical deterioration, graffiti or public drinking.

III. THE APPLICATION OF PREDICTIVE POLICING

In 2003, Gorr and Harries remarked that until then, crime forecasting was simply not feasible or at least not worth the effort [8]. Since then, the computerized collection of data has become standard in police departments, as well as monthly meetings to discuss strategic planning [10]. This allows the application of predictive algorithms in order to analyze data, forecast crimes and use this information to strategically position patrols. The predictive process is not supposed to change the overall policing methods, but to make them more effective [3].

Predictive policing can be used to forecast especially endangered areas, individuals or times, as well as people threatening to become offenders [1]. The practice of predictive methods - especially in the United States, the major field for predictive policing - has focused on property crimes such as residential burglary, that seems to be a particularly good case of application. As cited in II-B3, data supports the near-repeat theory, one of the most often applied theories in crime forecasting, in residential burglary [15]. Predictions based on individuals are delicate and may also be more prone to be affected by biases, these issues are being further discussed in chapter IV. Traditional police tactics have often been focusing on individuals and their crimes, forecasting techniques are of little use here, since the can only make predictions based on patterns but not on highly subjective decisions [8].

As shown in figure 1, one of the four steps in the predictive process is the execution of police operations. According to Perry et al., the inclusion of personal interventions based on analytic findings is crucial to the overall effectiveness and success of predictive policing. They define successful operations as having "top-level support, sufficient resources, automated systems to provide needed information, and assigned personnel with both the freedom to resolve crime problems and accountability for doing so", these comprehensive requirements show the necessity of personal actions based on predictions in order to actually decrease crime. [1]

With the availability of accurate short-term forecasts, police officers are able to allocate patrols in real-time, protecting neighborhoods especially at risk for being targeted, to shift resources between crime prevention and enforcement operations and to schedule vacations or training to trough crime months [8], [9], [12]. The identification of hot spots small enough to allow targeted operations facilitates strategical planning (see figure 2).

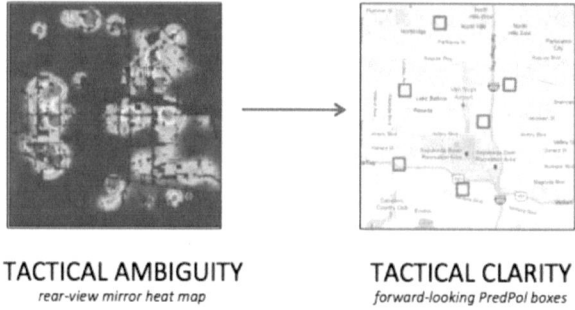

TACTICAL AMBIGUITY
rear-view mirror heat map

TACTICAL CLARITY
forward-looking PredPol boxes

Fig. 2. Predictive policing with hot spot identification and risk-terrain modeling can be of great use in strategical planning. By identifying not only the overall distribution of crimes but hot spots small enough to be easily monitored, resources can be deployed very effectively and the sole presence of police officers can prevent crime by creating a deterrence and suppression effect. [18]

IV. CRITIQUE AND DISCUSSION

An important thing to remember is that predictive policing only complements traditional policing methods but still requires humans to "connect the dots" [3]. The algorithms only predict the risk of future crimes happening at a specific time or place, but not the actual event. Police officers must pick out relevant patterns and then choose the correct way to react to the information obtained. [1]

One risk is, of course, that, over time, offenders may alter their behavior and habits in reaction to the developed model, and therefore evade detection. Hence forecasting algorithms should also be designed to be versatile and quickly adjust to new patterns and input. [3]

A point of criticism in predictive policing is that it might put some neighborhoods under general suspicion and permanent patrol, as well as generating self-fulfilling prophecies and prejudices among police officers. Police departments using crime forecasting methods have reacted with a great transparency towards the public and frequent blind control tests to evaluate the effects of the predictive models. [2], [3], [15]

V. CONCLUSION AND PROSPECT

Criminal offenses are usually results of affect and opportunity, however, they are also affected by seasonal, spatial and other variables, which means that they are subject to patterns. Providing that enough relevant and accurate data has been collected before, these patterns can be analyzed using a variety of theories and algorithms, and used to predict the time, place, victim or perpetrator of a future crime. The usage of computers for the analysis and prediction phase allows for quicker, more precise and maybe previously undetectable forecasts. However, predictions can only result in a reduction of crime if they are followed by concrete actions and measures. The presence of police officers has a powerful deterrent effect that can reduce future crimes [7].

Recent technologies and advancements in information systems and data mining have made computer-assisted predictive policing easier, more effective and worthwhile, even for smaller police departments [13], [15]. Forecasting methods need to be thoroughly tested and validated, like it is already happening for residential burglary use cases in the United States. The era of big data and the availability of a lot of information online (including on individuals, for example on social media) ensure a never-ending supply of data. Following the application of social media data to predict disease outbreaks or election results, Gerber et al. took the idea to police work by using spatiotemporally tagged Twitter data and the topics appearing there to improve existing prediction methods and forecast hit-and-run incidents [19], [20]. Information gained on social media can allow targeted monitoring of suspects announcing or boasting about crimes and therefore easily become centered on individuals. Therefore, the challenge is to efficiently analyze it and to put it to good use by acting on it while still maintaining constitutionality and the right to privacy.

Even though predictive policing can facilitate the policing process, Andrew Adams, professor of information ethics at Meji University remarks that "[t]he real world is messy and fuzzy [...] Predictions should never be taken as absolute reality" [3]. Therefore computational analyses and statistics should never replace traditional methods, but complement them and always be used with caution.

REFERENCES

[1] W. L. Perry, B. McInnis, C. C. Price, S. C. Smith, and J. S. Hollywood, Predictive Policing: The Role of Crime Forecasting in Law Enforcement Operations. RAND Corporation, 2013.

[2] B. Pearsall, "Predictive policing: The future of law enforcement?" National Institute of Justice Journal, vol. 266, pp. 16–19, 2010.

[3] S. Greengard, "Policing the future," Communications of the ACM, vol. 55, no. 3, pp. 19–21, 2012.

[4] C.-H. Yu, M. W. Ward, M. Morabito, and W. Ding, "Crime forecasting using data mining techniques," in 11th International Conference on Data Mining Workshops (ICDMW), 2011, pp. 779–786.

[5] W. Gorr and A. Olligschlaeger, "Crime hot spot forecasting: Modeling and comparative evaluation, summary," Rockville, MD.

[6] G. L. Kelling and C. M. Coles, Fixing broken windows: Restoring order and reducing crime in our communities, ser. A Touchstone book. New York: Simon & Schuster, 1997.

[7] W. J. Bratton, "Reducing crime through prevention not incarceration," Criminology & Public Policy, vol. 10, no. 1, pp. 63–68, 2011.

[8] W. Gorr and R. Harries, "Introduction to crime forecasting," International Journal of Forecasting, vol. 19, pp. 551–555, 2003.

[9] Y. Mu, W. Ding, M. Morabito, and D. Tao, "Empirical discriminative tensor analysis for crime forecasting," in Knowledge Science, Engineering and Management. Springer Berlin Heidelberg, 2011, pp. 293–304.

[10] W. Gorr, A. Olligschlaeger, and Y. Thompson, "Short-term forecasting of crime," International Journal of Forecasting, vol. 19, pp. 579–594, 2003.

[11] H. J. d. Knegt, F. van Langevelde, M. B. Coughenour, A. K. Skidmore, W. F. d. Boer, I. Heitkönig, N. M. Know, R. Slotow, C. van der Waal, and H. Prins, "Spatial autocorrelation and the scaling of species-environment relationships," Ecology, vol. 91, no. 8, pp. 2455–2565, 2010.

[12] J. J. Corcoran, I. D.Wilson, and J. A.Ware, "Predicting the geo-temporal variations of crime and disorder," International Journal of Forecasting, vol. 19, pp. 623–634, 2003.

[13] E. R. Groff and N. G. La Vigne, "Forecasting the future of predictive crime mapping," Crime Prevention Studies, vol. 13, pp. 29–58, 2002.

[14] M. B. Short, M. R. D'Orsogna, G. E. Pasour, P. J. Brantingham, A. L. Bertozzi, and L. B.

Chayes, "A statistical model of criminal behavior," Mathematical Models and Methods in Applied Sciences, vol. 18, pp. 1249–1267, 2008.

[15] A. G. Ferguson, "Predictive policing and reasonable suspicion," 62 Emory Law Journal, pp. 259–325, 2012.

[16] J. M. Caplan, L. W. Kennedy, and E. L. Piza, "Joint utility of eventdependent and environmental crime analysis techniques for violent crime forecasting," Crime & Delinquency, vol. 59, no. 2, pp. 243–270, 2013.

[17] G. O. Mohler, M. B. Short, P. J. Brantingham, F. P. Schoenberg, and G. E. Tita, "Self-exciting point process modeling of crime," Journal of the American Statistical Association, vol. 106, no. 493, pp. 100–108, 2011.

[18] PredPol, "What predpol is and what predpol is not," 19.11.2015. [Online]. Available: https://www.predpol.com/whatispredpol/

[19] M. S. Gerber, "Predicting crime using twitter and kernel density estimation," Decision Support Systems, vol. 61, pp. 115–125, 2014.

[20] X. Wang, M. S. Gerber, and D. E. Brown, "Automatic crime prediction using events extracted from twitter posts," in Social Computing, Behavioral - Cultural Modeling and Prediction, ser. Lecture Notes in Computer Science, D. Hutchison, T. Kanade, J. Kittler, J. M. Kleinberg, F. Mattern, J. C. Mitchell, M. Naor, O. Nierstrasz, C. Pandu Rangan, B. Steffen, M. Sudan, D. Terzopoulos, D. Tygar, M. Y. Vardi, G. Weikum, S. J. Yang, A. M. Greenberg, and M. Endsley, Eds. Berlin, Heidelberg: Springer Berlin Heidelberg, 2012, vol. 7227, pp. 231–238.